Positive

Tammy Griffith

Onwards and Upwards Publishers
www.onwardsandupwards.org

First edition published by Onwards and Upwards Publishers (2015).

Cover layout by LM Graphic Design. Printed in the UK. ISBN: 978-1-910197-98-1

Author's Note

Think positive…

Easier said than done sometimes.

Especially when we are in the midst of great challenges.

Experiences in my life have taught me that when life looks dark and there seems to be no solution, if we do not give up on God, He will continue to work in our lives. Either to change our situation for the better, or by bringing us the peace and strength we need to walk through the storm.

At the age of three I was diagnosed with a brain tumour, which was successfully surgically removed. Following surgery, I was left with several disabilities, but these did not stop me from achieving my goals.

In 2000, a scan revealed that there was a re-growth of the brain tumour, but its position meant further surgery was not possible.

I had a course of radiotherapy, however the tumour progressed into my spinal cord. The year's course of chemotherapy I was to undergo had to be aborted, as my condition continued to deteriorate. My treatment was discontinued, and I was discharged from hospital on a programme of palliative care.

After much prayer, and through events that I can only attribute to God's intervention, I was introduced to homeopathic and acupuncture therapies, which had an immediate positive effect.

I still have the tumour, and I daily live with the many challenges it places on my life, but I have continued to achieve so much.

Think Positive is a combination of the wisdom of others, and things life has taught me. I do not pretend to have yet mastered all the lessons contained within this book, and I know that it is easier to share them with others than it is to practise them oneself.

In reading this book, I hope that you will be reminded that a positive mental attitude is the key to surviving the challenges of life.

There are many situations that will affect our lives, which we have little or even no control over. The one thing we always have the power to control is our attitude. The attitude with which we choose to face life will determine whether we overcome our challenges or whether they overcome us.

With support I have been able to accomplish my goals, this book being one of them. When we choose to use our challenges as lesson books, we can achieve great things.

I'm not a lover of sports, but I do enjoy watching the Olympics and Paralympics. As I watch the latter, I am inspired by the ability and successes of the athletes, despite their day-to-day challenges, and their determination not to be held back. I am reminded that with God we are encouraged to expect the unexpected, because when we partner with Him, great things are promised.

May this book remind you that with God, the possibilities for success are truly endless.

Acknowledgements

Thank you to my mother and Peter for kindly taking the time to look over the manuscript and providing valuable feedback.

Thank you to those who have shared material or ideas with me, both of which have helped shape this book.

Contents

Positive Mental Attitude

"

Being happy is
an attitude
towards life...

Being happy
depends on you!

"

Your success
and happiness
in life depend
on the quality
of your
thoughts.

"

"

Your life will be
determined by
the way you
think.

"

"

Your attitude is
the control
centre of
your life.

"

" Attitude is everything: change your attitude... and you change your life! "

" Real happiness
is not
dependent on
what is going
on around you,
but what is
going on
within you. "

" Everyone wants
happiness,
no one wants
pain.
But you can't
have a rainbow
without a little
rain. "

Anonymous

" We should look at
what we have
today,
rather than
forever being
obsessed with
what we will
aquire tomorrow. "

" Happiness is a journey, not a destination. So stop waiting until... 'I have a spouse, a car, a new house, a new job'... to be happy. "

"

There is no
better time
than right now.

"

"

We each choose
our own path
in life...
We don't get to
choose the
obstacles we face
on the journey.

"

" Life isn't about
waiting for the
storms to pass.
It's about
learning to
dance in the
rain. "

" Don't wander through life just letting things happen to you, YOU make them happen.
Take the steering wheel of your life and choose your direction. "

"

Your future
happiness may
well depend on
your ability to
leave the past
behind.

"

Make peace
with your past,
so it won't
mess up your
present.

"

"

It's not who
you've been, but
who you are
becoming
that is most
important.

"

" Concentrate on
your potential and
set your course!
Forget what
everyone else has
going for them.
Find your rhythm
and style in life,
and LIVE. "

"

Dreams are
where you want
to go,
work is how you
get there.

"

Anonymous

" Happy are those
who dream
dreams,
and are willing
to pay the price
to make them
come true. "

Anonymous

" Don't dismiss your
(or anyone else's)
dreams.
To be without
dreams is to be
without hope.

To be without hope
is to be without
purpose. "

"

Don't let the
pain
of one season
in your life
destroy the joy
of all the rest.

"

" Your life today is more than what happened yesterday; it's about what you do with yesterday's experiences. "

"

Every ending is
a new beginning.
The completion of
one journey is the
start of a new one.

So don't waste time
despairing over what
you must leave behind.
Invest time preparing
for what you are about
to enter.

"

The Keys to Success

"

Success is not a
destination...
It is a journey.

"

"

Success:
Willing to do
what the
average person
is not
willing to do.

"

Anonymous

"

No masterpiece
was ever
created by a
lazy artist.

"

Anonymous

"

You can only
get out of life
as much as you
put in.

"

"

Success is:

5% inspiration,

95% perspiration.

"

" Take your
challenges
and turn them into
opportunities -
in the middle
of every difficulty
lie many
unexplored
possibilities. "

" The frustrations,
pressures and enemies
we meet in the pursuit
of our goals
are not obstacles to us
achieving them...

They are merely
stepping stones which
we must inevitably
cross on our journey. "

" Tough times
do not have to
break our spirit.

They can
shape us,
challenge us,
and help us
to grow. "

" Your problems
don't cause
your actions.

Your problems
simply reveal
who you are on
the inside. "

"

Adversity introduces a man to himself.

Anonymous

" You are defeated,
not when you fall
and fail to reach
your goals,
but when you
give up trying to
attain them.
"

" No matter the
dark holes the
circumstances of
life may
lead you down,
never give up
striving for
something better. "

" Success is failure
turned inside out
and upside down.

Life's greatest
lessons can come
from our greatest
failures. "

" The willingness to fail gives you the freedom to succeed... Failure is often the father of success. "

"

Turn your
misfortunes
into
opportunities.

"

"

Just as
no success is
ever final,
so failure is
never the end.

"

Stephen Rivers

"

If you fall and
stay down,
life will pass
you by.

"

"

You can tell
how big a
person is
by what it
takes to
discourage
them.

"

" Life's real
failure is when
you do not
realise how
close you were
to success when
you gave up. "

Anonymous

" Disappointments in
life are
bound to happen.
Doors we thought
were wide open
close unexpectedly,
relationships
we thought
would last forever
come to an end,
dreams we cherish
do not come true... "

" Someone wisely
said:

'When God says
no, it's because
there is a
greater yes in
the future.' **"**

" If we do not give up in the face of disappointments, each one becomes a stepping stone to something better. "

" Trust in the Lord with all your heart. Never rely on what you think you know.

Remember the Lord in everything you do, and he will show you the right way. **"**

Proverbs 3:5-6, The Holy Bible (GNB)

Confronting Tomorrow

66

You can't
change the past,
but you can
ruin the present
by worrying
over the future.

99

"

Never borrow
from the future.

If you worry about
what may happen
tomorrow and it
doesn't happen, you
have worried in vain.
Even if it does happen,
you'll have to
worry twice.

"

"

A little dose of
faith goes a
long way to
curing a whole
load of worries.

"

" The Lord himself
watches over you!
The Lord stands
beside you as your
protective shade ...
The Lord keeps
watch over you as
you come and go,
both now and
forever. "

Psalm 121:5,8, The Holy Bible (NLT)

"

Worry is like a
rocking chair;
it gives you
something to
do, but it
doesn't get you
anywhere.

"

"

Worry makes
our days long,
and our lives
short.

"

"
So don't worry
about tomorrow,
for tomorrow will
bring its own
worries.
Today's trouble is
enough for today.
"

Matthew 6:34, The Holy Bible (NLT)

" When life
pushes you to
your wits' end,
you'll find that
God is
already there. "

"

Leave all your
worries with
him, because he
cares for you.

"

1 Peter 5:7, The Holy Bible (GNB)

" What needs to come through to a world in panic is the Good News that the Prince of Peace has made provision for ETERNAL PEACE. "

"...he will be called Wonderful Counsellor, Mighty God, Everlasting Father, Prince of Peace."

Isaiah 9:6b, The Holy Bible

"

God sees our
tomorrows before
they become
our todays.
Never fear to
submit an
unknown future
into His hands.

"

"

...your Father
knows exactly
what you need
even before you
ask him!

"

Matthew 6:8b, The Holy Bible (NLT)

" Every evening I turn my worries over to God. He's going to be up all night anyway! "

Mary C. Crowley

"
Everything can
change in the
blink of an eye.
But don't
worry,
God never
blinks.
"

Incomparable Worth

"

So don't be
afraid; you are
worth more
than many
sparrows.

"

Matthew 10:31, The Holy Bible

" Once you've
discovered yourself,
learn to be happy
with who you are.
If you cannot accept
yourself, you cannot
expect anyone else to.
God made you special
and unique,
bask in that truth. "

"

Don't undermine
your worth by
comparing yourself
with others.

It is because we are
different that each
of us is special.

"

" Look at the birds of the air; they do not sow or reap or store away in barns, and yet your heavenly Father feeds them. Are you not much more valuable than they? "

Matthew 6:26, The Holy Bible

" You were created
in God's image, and
God doesn't make
junk! So hold your
head high, and
walk with pride.
You are a
PRIZED
POSSESSION. "

"

Seek to change
what you can
and accept
what you can't.

"

" To compare yourself with
others who you think are
more intelligent and
beautiful or who have
more wealth and courage
than you do, draws you
into a soul-destroying
game. A game that is
impossible for you to win.
Who would compare a cat
with a sunset,
or a homemade cake
with a song? "

" Each of us is
unique,
incomparable;

and that is
what makes life
interesting. "

" Know that the
Lord is God.
It is he
who made us,
and we are his;
we are his people,
the sheep of his
pasture. "

Psalm 100:3, The Holy Bible

Priceless Wisdom

66

The doorstep to
the temple of
wisdom is a
knowledge of
our own
ignorance.

99

Benjamin Franklin

" Don't run through life so fast that you forget, not only where you have been, but also where you are going. "

"

Life is
not a race,
but a journey to
be savoured
each step
of the way.

"

"

Enjoy life now -
it has an
expiration date.

"

" Burn the
special candles,
use the nice sheets,
wear the
fancy clothes.
You don't have to
save them for a
special occasion.
Today is special. "

" Yesterday is
ashes.

Tomorrow is
green wood.

Only today does
the fire burn
brightly. "

Eskimo proverb

"

Don't let life slip through your fingers, by living in the past or the future.

"

" By living your
life one day
at a time,
you live all
the days of
your life
to the full. "

" Lost wealth
may be replaced
by industry.
Lost knowledge
by study.
Lost health
by temperance
or medicine.
But lost time is
gone forever. "

Samuel Smiles

"

One thing I
can't recycle is
wasted time.

"

"

Do not
squander time,
for that's the
stuff life is
made of.

"

Benjamin Franklin

" Enjoy the little things in life...

For one day you'll look back and realise they were the big things. "

" Never get tired of doing little things for others. Sometimes those little things occupy the biggest part of their hearts. **"**

"

Don't compare
your life to
others'.
You have no
idea what their
journey has
been like.

"

"

Life isn't tied
with a bow, but
it is still a gift.

"

**" THE SERENITY
PRAYER**

God, grant me the
serenity to accept
the things I
cannot change,
courage to change the
things I can,
and the wisdom to
know the difference. **"**

You are
Not Alone

"

For God has
said, 'I will
never leave you
or abandon
you.'

"

Hebrews 13:5, The Holy Bible (ISV)

"

Life is trying
sometimes -
in fact,
most of the time -
but God has promised
to always be with us.

So do not become
discouraged,
do not become afraid,
you need never
struggle alone.

"

" God is our refuge and strength, always ready to help in times of trouble. "

Psalm 46:1, The Holy Bible (NLT)

"

God joins us in
the midst of our
storms.

"

"

Christ offers
rest from the
crushing burdens of
guilt, anxiety,
selfishness, stress
and hostility
that so often take
the joy out of life.

"

"

Come to me,
all you who are
weary and
burdened,
and I will
give you rest.

"

Matthew 11:28, The Holy Bible

" God loves you;
and nothing can
separate you
from that love.
Whatever
situations you
face, God has
your back. "

"

If God is for us,
who can ever be
against us?

"

Romans 8:31b, The Holy Bible (NLT)

66 When we put our trust in God, we need not be intimidated by the words of others. When placed before Him, their intimidating words and great strength fade into insignificance. 99

" The Lord is my
light and my
salvation -
so why should I
be afraid?
The Lord is my
fortress, protecting
me from danger,
so why should I
tremble? "

Psalm 27:1, The Holy Bible (NLT)

" When the odds are
against us,
and things seem
impossible,
remember that
there is a God
who does not have
IMPOSSIBLE
in His vocabulary. "

"

With God your
future is full of
endless
possibilities.

"

" This is how much God
loved the world:
He gave his Son,
his one and only Son.

And this is why:
so that no one need
be destroyed;
by believing in him,
anyone can have a
whole and lasting life. **"**

John 3:16, The Holy Bible (MSG)

66 God didn't go to all
the trouble of
sending his Son
merely to point
an accusing finger,
telling the world
how bad it was.
He came to help,
to put the world
right again. 99

John 3:17, The Holy Bible (MSG)

"

He whose plans
never fail has a
plan for you.

" I alone know the plans I have for you, plans to bring you prosperity and not disaster, plans to bring about the future you hope for. "

Jeremiah 29:11, The Holy Bible (GNB)

"

God doesn't sleep.
He doesn't
take holidays.
He doesn't
take breaks.
No one can be there
to protect you
all the time,
but God can.

We can put all our
hope in Him.

"

The Keys to Happiness

"

We should
spend less time
trying to
LOOK GOOD
and a lot more
time actually
DOING GOOD.

"

" Anger is an acid
that can do
more harm to the
vessel in which
it is stored,
than to anything
on which
it is poured. "

Mark Twain

"

Anger is a
condition
in which
the tongue
works faster
than the mind.

"

"

The heaviest
thing you can
carry is a
grudge.

"

...be kind
to each other,
tenderhearted,
forgiving one
another,
just as God
through Christ
has forgiven you. "

Ephesians 4:32, The Holy Bible (NLT)

"
You cannot
change the world...

but you can
change yourself
for the better;
and in improving
yourself,
you can touch others
in life-changing ways.

❝ Be kind to others, for
God loves them just as
much as He loves you.

They may not
dress like you,
talk like you,
or live the same way
you do,
but He still
loves us all. **❞**

" You only have a
lifetime to make
a difference.
Make the most
of it,
leave your mark -
touch somebody's
life. "

"

ASPIRE
to
INSPIRE
before you
EXPIRE.

"

"

Don't
underestimate
a small
kindness.
You never know
how big it is
to someone else.

"

" It is one of the most beautiful compensations in life that no man can sincerely try to help another without helping himself. "

Ralph Waldo Emerson

"

So in
everything,
do to others
what you would
have them
do to you...

"

Matthew 7:12, The Holy Bible

" Don't take people
for granted.
A word of
encouragement
or thanks
can make
someone's day.
MAKE SOMEONE
SMILE! "

" Don't let a small thing blind you from seeing someone's good qualities...
We all have some annoying habits. While we work on improving our own, we need to overlook them in others. "

"

Be patient
with others,
each one of us
is a work in
progress.

"

"

Our ultimate
purpose is
to be loved,
and to love in
return.

"

" The three
most worthy
pursuits in life:

Love God.
Love others.
Be yourself. "

" ...'Love the Lord your God with all your heart and with all your soul and with all your mind.' This is the first and greatest commandment. And the second is like it: 'Love your neighbour as yourself.' "

Matthew 22:37-39, The Holy Bible

" Our fears for today, our worries about tomorrow, or where we are - high above the sky, or in the deepest ocean - nothing will ever be able to separate us from the love of God demonstrated by our Lord Jesus Christ when he died for us. "

Romans 8:38b-39, The Holy Bible (TLB)

"

GOD LOVES YOU

Regardless of
anything you've
done or failed to do.

"

"

God's love is like
the ocean:
you can see its
beginnings but not
its end.

"

Wisdom from Above

"

You can buy
education,
but wisdom is
a gift from God.

"

"

Everyone
thinks of
changing the
world, but no
one thinks of
changing
himself.

"

Leo Tolstoy

" If you want to
see change in
the world, there
is no better
place to start
than with
yourself. "

" We do not have to
strive to be
somebody great.
Rather we should
strive to do things
that make a
great difference
to the lives of
others around us. "

"

TEAM =

T-ogether
E-veryone
A-chieves
M-ore

"

"

There is no 'I'
in TEAM,
but there is no
team without
individuals.

"

"

As iron
sharpens iron,
so one person
sharpens
another.

"

Proverbs 27:17, The Holy Bible

"

Teamwork
divides the task
and multiplies
the success.

"

" Two people can achieve what one cannot.

People are better, braver, wiser, and more effective as a team than they are alone. "

" Two are better than
one, because they have
a good return
for their labor:
If either of them falls
down, one can help
the other up.
But pity anyone who
falls and has no one to
help them up. "

Ecclesiastes 4:9-10, The Holy Bible

66 Also, if two lie down together, they will keep warm. But how can one keep warm alone? Though one may be overpowered, two can defend themselves. A cord of three strands is not quickly broken. **99**

Ecclesiastes 4:11-12, The Holy Bible

"

Friends are like
balloons;
once you let
them go,
you might not
get them back.

"

"

Don't let a little
dispute injure
a great
friendship.

"

" Learn from other
people's mistakes,
from their lost
opportunities, and let
the special people in
your life know how
much you love and
appreciate them.

Life without them
would be very lonely.

" Wisdom is,
and starts with,
the humility to
accept the fact that
you don't have all
the right answers,
and the courage to
learn to ask the
right questions. "

Anonymous

"

Pride comes
before
destruction,
and an
arrogant spirit
before a fall.

Proverbs 16:18, The Holy Bible (HCSB)

His Healing Touch

"

Earth has no sorrow that heaven cannot heal.

"

Thomas Moore

"

God can do
wonders with
a broken heart,
if you give him
all the pieces.

"

" There is only one problem that God cannot fix; the problem that we make bigger than Him. "

"

GOD SAYS:

I want to
help you.
All you have
to do is ask.

"

" When they
call on me,
I will answer;
I will be with
them in trouble.
I will rescue
and honor
them. "

Psalm 91:15, The Holy Bible (NLT)

"

Prayer is one of
the best gifts
we receive.
There is no cost,
but a lot of
rewards.

"

"

When the world
pushes you to
your knees,
you're in the
perfect position
to pray.

"

"

Being happy is
an attitude
towards life...

Being happy
depends on you!

"

"

The best
mathematical
equation:

1 cross + 3 nails
= 4given

"

"

God loves us
enough to
accept us
as we are.
God loves us too
much to leave
us the same.

"

" Whoever dwells in the shelter of the Most High will rest in the shadow of the Almighty... He will cover you with his feathers, and under his wings you will find refuge... "

Psalm 91:1,4, The Holy Bible

" In the midst of our
storms, God is there,
willing to give us a
peace that defies our
circumstances.
To trust God to give us
that peace is the
greatest challenge,
to receive and
experience it is the
greatest joy. "